The Camping Trip
That Changed America

THEODORE ROOSEVELT, JOHN MUIR,
and our NATIONAL PARKS

by
BARB ROSENSTOCK

Illustrated by
MORDICAI GERSTEIN

Dial Books for Young Readers AN IMPRINT OF PENGUIN GROUP (USA) INC.

For Danny and Jeff
—B.R.

For Joan Raines,
thank you for everything.
You are a treasure!
—M.G.

DIAL BOOKS FOR YOUNG READERS
A division of Penguin Young Readers Group

——————————— Published by the Penguin Group ———————————

Penguin Group (USA) Inc., 375 Hudson Street, New York, New York 10014, U.S.A. • Penguin Group (Canada), 90 Eglinton Avenue
East, Suite 700, Toronto, Ontario, Canada M4P 2Y3 (a division of Pearson Penguin Canada Inc.) • Penguin Books Ltd, 80 Strand,
London WC2R 0RL, England • Penguin Ireland, 25 St Stephen's Green, Dublin 2, Ireland (a division of Penguin Books Ltd) •
Penguin Group (Australia), 250 Camberwell Road, Camberwell, Victoria 3124, Australia (a division of Pearson Australia Group Pty
Ltd) • Penguin Books India Pvt Ltd, 11 Community Centre, Panchsheel Park, New Delhi—110 017, India • Penguin Group (NZ), 67
Apollo Drive, Rosedale, Auckland 0632, New Zealand (a division of Pearson New Zealand Ltd) • Penguin Books (South Africa) (Pty)
Ltd, 24 Sturdee Avenue, Rosebank, Johannesburg 2196, South Africa • Penguin Books Ltd, Registered Offices: 80 Strand, London
WC2R 0RL, England

Library of Congress Cataloging-in-Publication Data
Rosenstock, Barbara.
The camping trip that changed America/by Barbara Rosenstock; illustrated by Mordicai Gerstein.
p. cm.
ISBN 978-0-8037-3710-5 (hardcover)
1. Roosevelt, Theodore, 1858–1919—Travel—California—Yosemite Valley—Juvenile literature. 2. Muir, John, 1838–1914—Juvenile
literature. 3. Yosemite National Park (Calif.)—History—Juvenile literature. 4. National parks and reserves—United States—History—
Juvenile literature. 5. Environmentalism—United States—History—Juvenile literature. I. Gerstein, Mordicai, ill. II. Title.
E757.R93 2012   979.4′47—dc23
2011021927

Published in the United States by Dial Books for Young Readers,
a division of Penguin Young Readers Group
345 Hudson Street, New York, New York 10014
www.penguin.com/youngreaders

Manufactured in China • First Edition

THEODORE ROOSEVELT

JOHN MUIR

Teedie *and* Johnnie

didn't have much in common—but they shared a love of the outdoors. They both loved a good story, too. And that was enough to change America.

YOSEMITE

THEODORE ROOSEVELT'S family had called him Teedie since he was a boy. He grew up in one of the oldest, richest families in New York City. Teedie was short and brawny, with a fashionable mustache. He loved the outdoors: hunting, fishing, and riding horses. He attended law school before becoming a politician. Theodore Roosevelt became the youngest president of the United States, and lived with his wife and six children in the White House in Washington, D.C.

J OHN MUIR'S family had called him Johnnie since he was a boy. He grew up in the Midwest, the son of poor immigrant farmers. Johnnie was tall, thin, and quiet, with shaggy hair that curled into a long beard. He loved the outdoors: studying, sketching, and writing about plants. He hiked the American wilderness alone and wrote about his travels. John Muir became a world-famous naturalist and protector of wild places with a special love for the Yosemite wilderness near his farmhouse in California.

Teedie settled into his favorite chair. He loved to end the day reading. Tonight, he chose a book by John Muir. Muir's adventures in California's Sierra Mountains sounded just about perfect to the busy president.

It was strange then, when Muir ended his story by asking for help . . . help for trees! He said the wild forests were vanishing. He called on the government to save them.

The president thought about those mountain forests for a long time. Most people, even his own experts, thought America had so much wilderness it couldn't ever be used up!

Was John Muir right? Could the forests disappear? How could the government help? As president, Teedie needed answers.

Roosevelt wrote John Muir a letter. The president was planning a long trip to the western states. He asked John Muir to take him camping in Calfornia's Yosemite wilderness at the end of the trip. If America's forests needed help, the president wanted to see those trees for himself.

Roosevelt's train stopped in cities and towns along its route toward Yosemite. At each stop, bands played, officials gave speeches, and people crowded the platform to catch a glimpse of the popular president the newspapers nicknamed "Teddy."

The train reached the end of the line in the small town of Raymond, California, about thirty miles outside the Yosemite wilderness.

When he found men sending his baggage to the best hotel in town, Roosevelt shouted, "By George, I'm going camping! Pack me one small sack!"

Along with a crowd of officials, townspeople, newspapermen, and photographers, John Muir waited to meet the president.

Teedie shook Johnnie's hand, "I've enjoyed your stories, Muir."

The president spoke a few words to the crowd. Then he joined Muir in a waiting stagecoach. They bumped along the road to Yosemite. Another stop. More speeches.

Muir was growing impatient. Didn't the president want to see the wilderness?

Then Roosevelt's voice boomed, "Enough pictures, folks. I'd like to see the rest of this country in peace."

The president sent his men ahead to set up camp. Leaving the shocked crowd behind, Teedie and Johnnie rode off alone.

"*I feel like a runaway schoolboy!*" Teedie laughed as his horse galloped along.

They stopped near a family of giant sequoias in the Mariposa Grove. Surrounded by the trees of this ancient forest, for once Teedie was quiet. When he looked up, he couldn't see the treetops. The sequoias soared straight to the heavens.

"These trees grew up when the Egyptians built the pyramids," said Johnnie. "They are the largest living things on earth. They never stop growing—unless they are cut down."

That night, under the branches of a towering sequoia called the Grizzly Giant, Teedie lay on the forty thick wool blankets his men prepared.

Johnnie made a bed from some branches and wrapped himself in an old cloth from his sack. He told Teedie the funny story of meeting his first bear.

I once saw a bear in a meadow. Now, bears are shy creatures, so I jumped out from behind a tree just to see him run away.

The bear looks up. I ran toward him shouting and waving.

I finally stopped or I would've run right into him! The bear rose up, put his claws on a log between us, and glared.

Teedie laughed. "Was it a grizzly bear?" he asked.

Johnnie shook his head. "The only grizzly left in Yosemite today is this old tree. Hunters shot the last bear a few years ago."

I'd made a big mistake about shy bears. I had to stand perfectly still for hours or I would've been his dinner!

Finally, the bear rambled off, checking back over his hind end to make sure I stayed put.

That bear and I were both scared and embarrassed, but I tell you it was the bear that had the better manners!

Under the trees, Teedie and Johnnie slept.

The next day Teedie and Johnnie rode higher into the mountains, trading stories the way friends do. As the horses plowed through drifts of snow, they reached a peak called Glacier Point.

"Glaciers carved this whole valley," said Johnnie, spreading his arms. He lay down on a slab of granite and inched along on his back to show how a massive river of slow-moving ice carved the rock beneath them millions of years before.

They camped high above the valley floor. Johnnie made the president a bed of branches and they settled near the fire for warmth. Johnnie began his story, "This whole continent is a great garden . . ."

Before the beginning of time, ancient seas covered the land churning the rocks into soil.

As the seas dried, volcanoes sculpted mountains and valleys,

glaciers carved rivers and created plains.

My children should see this place," said Teedie.
"I hope it is still here for them," said Johnnie.

Trees and flowers grew
into forests and meadows.

Wild birds and beasts
filled the land.

Everywhere nature sang her
melody. Can you hear it?

Under the trees, Teedie and Johnnie slept.

May 17, 1903

Overnight a storm blew in, spreading five inches of fresh snow. Teedie and Johnnie woke under a coverlet of white flakes. They shook themselves off like two old grizzly bears.

"Bully!" said Teedie, stretching.

"What a glorious day!"

On horseback, Muir and Roosevelt rode down into
the famous Yosemite Valley. The granite formations towered above
them. They passed the sheared cliff of Half Dome and the fierce face of
El Capitan rising from the valley floor.

On their last night together, John Muir talked to the president about life in the wilderness. People were destroying wild land to make money from it. Ranchers cleared forests, prospectors mined gold, and companies planned to build hotels and shops throughout the valley. There was no one to stop them.

"If they keep building, the wilderness won't last another ten years," said
Muir.

"How can I help?" asked the president.

"Keep it wild," Muir said, "and protect it forever."

Together, Teedie and Johnnie
imagined a different future for America.

What if everyone owned the wilderness?

What if both rich and poor
could spend time out in the open?

What if we could save the forests
for all the children to come?

America's Wilderness, 1903 and beyond

Teedie left Johnnie in Yosemite and headed back home. His time in the
forest turned the outdoor-loving president into one of nature's fiercest
protectors. Roosevelt pushed Congress to pass laws saving the wilderness. He
failed at first, but that didn't stop him. He created national parks, wildlife
sanctuaries, and national forests. With John Muir's spirit as his guide,
Theodore Roosevelt saved more wild land than any president in history.

Teedie and Johnnie never spent any time together again. Teedie traveled
the world but called the night of the snowstorm "the one day of my life that
I will always remember with pleasure." Johnnie felt the same. He wrote
that he "fairly fell in love" with the president.

They exchanged personal letters for the rest of their lives.

John Muir lies under the incense cedar trees he planted near his home in Martinez, California.

Theodore Roosevelt lies beneath the sugar maples in the Roosevelt family plot in Oyster Bay, New York.

For all time, under the trees, Teedie and Johnnie sleep—and their shared spirit protects our wilderness forever.

Author's Note

"**Any fool can destroy trees.** They cannot run away, and if they could, they would still be destroyed—chased and hunted down as long as fun or a dollar could be got . . . It took more than three thousand years to make some of the trees in these Western woods—God has cared for these trees, saved them from drought, disease, avalanches . . . but he cannot save them from fools—only Uncle Sam can do that!"
—John Muir, *Our National Parks*, 1901

"**Lying out at night** under those giant Sequoias was lying in . . . a temple grander than any human architect could by any possibility build, and I hope for the preservation of the groves of giant trees simply because it would be a shame to our civilization to let them disappear . . . We are not building this country of ours for a day. It is to last through the ages."
—Theodore Roosevelt, May 19, 1903

This story is based in truth. Theodore Roosevelt wrote John Muir a letter on March 14, 1903, asking Muir to take him camping—"I do not want anyone with me but you, and I want to drop politics absolutely for four days and just be out in the open with you." Muir almost refused. He was tired of being a tour guide for people who didn't understand the need to protect wild lands. Ranchers, farmers, and builders felt free to develop and destroy wilderness, even those parts protected by the state—and no one stopped them. At sixty-five years old, the well-known Muir was traveling the world researching and speaking about preserving wilderness; the last thing he wanted to do was to take another noisy politician camping. Friends persuaded him that the outdoor-loving Roosevelt might be convinced to create strong federal laws to protect wild forests forever.

There is little historical record of exactly what happened between the two men during the time they spent in camp. Except for three men who went along as packers and cooks, and brief encounters with reporters, Theodore Roosevelt and John Muir rode or hiked on their own for much of the time. They did sleep outdoors, under the trees, even in the spring snowstorm.

Roosevelt returned to Washington passionate about protecting America's wilderness. He used an act that was designed to protect small historic structures to put large tracts of land under federal protection by declaring them National Monuments. There was no vote. He declared the first 18 National Monuments, including Devils Tower, the Petrified Forest, Mount Olympus, and the Grand Canyon. Under Theodore Roosevelt, the government founded the first 55 bird sanctuaries and game preserves, added 148 million acres to the National Forest and doubled the number of National Parks.

Since both Roosevelt and Muir were avid readers and writers, I imagined that it was the stories Muir told that helped convince the president of the value of saving America's wild lands. The imagined dialogue is in keeping with ideas from the letters of Muir and Roosevelt, Muir's *The Eight Wilderness Discovery Books*, as well as Charlie Leidig's first person account of the trip and California newspapers of the time. The story of Yosemite and the rest of America's wild places started before the beginning of time and will continue into the future through all of us.

THANKS TO:

Tom Bopp; Linda Eade, Yosemite Research Library; Tad Shay, John Muir National Site; Lee Stetson; Shan Sutton, University of the Pacific Library; and Amy Verone, Sagamore Hill.

SOURCES INCLUDE:

"Great Reception for Pres. Roosevelt," *Oakland Tribune*, May 29, 1903.

Hata, Donald. *With Theodore Roosevelt and John Muir in Yosemite.* Los Angeles: The Westerners Brand Book, 1974.

Leidig, Charlie. *Report of President Roosevelt's Visit in May, 1903,* Yosemite Library, unpublished.

Muir, John. *The Eight Wilderness Discovery Books.* Seattle: The Mountaineers, reprinted 1992.

"Roosevelt Pitches his Camp near Bleak Sentinel Dome in Snow Storm," *San Francisco Chronicle*, May 17, 1903.